The Memoir

of a

Student

The Memoir of a Student

Published 2025 by Frederick David
Copyright © Frederick David
ISBN: 978-1-916544-84-0

All rights reserved. No part of this publication may be reproduced or transmitted in any form or by any means, electronic or mechanical, including photography, recording, or any information storage or retrieval system without permission in writing from Frederick David. The book is sold subject to the condition that it shall not, by way of trade or otherwise, be lent, copied, altered, resold or otherwise circulated without Frederick David's prior consent.

Publishing Information

Design & publishing services
provided by JM Agency

www.jm.agency
Kerry, Ireland

The Memoir

of a

Student

Communication: A Personal Opinion

Frederick David

To the university.

The author is pleased to acknowledge the outstanding contribution of himself to the preparation of this book.

*To learn without thinking is fatal
but to think without learning is just as bad.*

— **Confucius**

Imagination decides everything.

— **Blaise Pascal**

CONTENTS

FIRST WEEK	13
SECOND WEEK	27
THIRD WEEK	41
FOURTH WEEK	49
FIFTH WEEK	61
SIXTH WEEK	69
SEVENTH WEEK	79
EIGHTH WEEK	87
NINTH WEEK	97
TENTH WEEK	97
ELEVENTH WEEK	97
ABOUT THE AUTHOR	111

FIRST WEEK

What is communication? The exact definition of this frequently used word is not so apparent as it conveys a vast and vague idea. Is it merely an exchange of raw data between two points or is it something broader or less straightforward? Why do we communicate? What do we computer studies students have to gain from the study of this subject? How good a communicator am I? It was with these questions in mind that I sat down for the first time that afternoon in a lecture hall, in the midst of others who no doubt had similar queries, without really knowing what to expect.

On entering the auditorium, the symmetrical arrangement of the tables reminded me of an examination room, and that did nothing to dispel the sense of confusion I already felt prior to coming here. Eventually, four dynamic lecturers made their appearance: Anna, Chris, Mike, and Valerie, the team leader. Seeing cheerful faces was reassuring and Chris clearly told us that we were not sitting for an exam, although it might look like it. This opening stage of building up rapport was noteworthy, as the ability to reassure people could prove to be a useful interpersonal communication skill for the future.

While the course details were outlined, it became clear that we would be expected to interact with each other. We would tackle many aspects of communication, such as the written report, body language and video presentations. We would be expected to speak in front of an audience. *Oh dear*. I could not help an initial feeling of apprehension because if there is something I dread, it is public speaking. On such occasions my stomach ties itself in knots, and, seeing the faces of many others, I was not the only one manifesting those ganglionic symptoms. Giving presentations would be the *bête noire* of the course.

Some would suggest that the most effective remedy against a phobia is to confront its cause. In other words, if one is afraid of speaking in public, one should do it intensively and continuously until the fear is gone. That sounds too drastic a medicine for me. I know that we are encouraged to improve our weak skills, but if I heed this advice, I will surely end up with an ulcer. Instead of following such allopathic treatment, with the unwanted side effects, I personally favour a homeopathic therapy of small, tiny, diluted doses to cure this minor complaint and, hence, I will try to keep a low profile and tactfully expose myself to the minimum. Pharmacovigilance, the science concerned with adverse drug reactions, is a crucial factor when selecting appropriate medication to ensure the best outcome from an antidote in a clinical trial. There is no placebo response here, as this is no sugar pill.

For the first task of the afternoon, we were each assigned a unique digit in order to play a 'game' – if I may use this term. The aim of which was for us to locate a corresponding classmate by any means possible. Here we were, with just a numeric constant for reference. We had lost our identities. I felt like a solitary byte, a simple subscript in the middle of a multidimensional array. I was not a person but an integer, pseudo-randomly generated by a hashing algorithm, that had to discover a certain discrete value to axiomatically integrate, before interviewing it with a set of questions for communication to potentially increase exponentially. Faced with such a complex arithmetic problem, I wondered whether this could be solved using number theory, dealing as it does with issues of mathematical certainty, the foundation of all science. Could I also apply game theory, where statistical logic is used in determining successful strategies, consequently aiding decision-making through defining available options? And, by making reliable point estimates, I would reduce any residuals.

How good was the probability of me finding a possible solution to the given equation? Was the expression fundamentally a function of chance? Or was another algebraic formula required to calculate the additional unknown parametric variables? Would it not be great if the relevant statistics could be demonstrated as a normal distribution graph, with all observations under the curve within one, two, and three standard deviations of the mean – the positive square root of the variance describing the dispersion, or spread, of the data set – easily assessed using the empirical rule? Should I also dwell on moments for grouped data, distinct constants used to describe certain characteristics of the graphical representation, such as skewness (the extent of asymmetry), and kurtosis (the state of flatness or 'peakedness'), with an assumption of a mesokurtic chart? Or must I just concentrate on numerical descriptive measures of central tendency, such as the mean and median? Would computing the correlation coefficient for the sampling and evaluating its percentile ranking and interquartile range arguably not optimise the inference-making process? Also, can a meaningful estimation not be obtained from a relative frequency histogram for quantitative data, where locating the position of the mode within a modal class is an important and useful indicator? Likewise, could permutations and combinations not contribute to a better prediction of the probable single outcome within the possibility space of the experiment?

And what about conducting a test of the hypothesis, identifying the critical values dividing both the rejection and non-rejection regions, thus deciding whether to accept or reject the null hypothesis, with convincing evidence, in favour of the alternative hypothesis as related to the purpose of the research? Furthermore, how could I detect any potential outliers, output that is usually large or small relative to the other amounts and clearly generated by different procedures from the rest of the data, attributable to diverse causes, with a prevailing propensity to distort results? What were the degrees of freedom? What was the goodness of fit? To minimise inconsistencies, could a method such as propagation of uncertainty – ambiguities and observational errors due to measurement limitations caused by instrument imprecision or misreading replicated from one set of variables onto another – be derived analytically in explicit form? Therefore, knowing the discrepancy and distinguishing between the correct figure and the approximation, and defining the confidence interval, or interval estimate, describing the range within which the true value of a parameter lies, along with a percentage–the significance level – specifying how sure I am of the conclusion. Accuracy – trueness and exactness – was of the utmost importance. As well as irrefutable information, mathematical proof, absolute and devoid of any doubt, built on infallible logic, was necessary to answer all these questions.

Though it seemed odd at first, I must admit this was an original idea and it was getting us very excited. It was an unusual and innovative plan for getting to know each other and making friends. Students were gesticulating and shouting. Some even stood on tables yelling out their figure in search of a partner. But I still had to determine with certainty the sample space containing the set of all possible sample points – the basic outcomes of this experiment – the probabilities of which must be between zero and one, and must all sum to one. And the probability of the event – a specific collection of all potential results – of me meeting a perfect counterpart could be calculated by summing the probabilities of the elements in the range of values for the occurrence of interest. Well, that was simple and explained everything. Notwithstanding the theory put forward and used as the basis for argument, I now needed some practical and concrete conclusion, as I was most concerned with its application. And so, after much statistical thinking, I got a marker, and I wrote my numerical symbol on a sheet of paper, literally stuck it on my chest and off I went, wandering away like a dangling pointer, free to roam at will within the memory area defined by the lecture theatre, but knowing that, thanks to the universal law of gravitation, I was bound to be attracted by some other particle. Auspiciously, the general theory of relativity, providing an alternate and more detailed explanation of gravity, had helped me better understand this gravitational pull effect. What an utter disorder and total chaos from which, a big bang, some sudden forceful beginning, could unfold and expand. Providentially, not the destructive cataclysmic change evoking a *Götterdämmerung*, a total destruction characterised by extreme commotion and violence.

We were a mass of radioactive isotopes accelerating frenetically within a reactor chamber. We moved around frantically, with increasing velocity, like vibrating nuclear fragments propagated in a magnetic field, smashing into each other, rebounding and spinning off in all entropic orbital directions, before having our rotational trajectory ended by the force of gravity. As oppositely charged ionic substances jostling one another, our ceaseless random motion produced enough kinetic energy, released as heat, for us to absorb and become atoms in an excited state. And I, an atomic nucleus, carried a positive charge and tended to repel other protons electrically. I knew that for fusion to happen, I had to move with sufficient speed to overcome this repulsion and approach the other body to within a short enough distance for attraction of the strong nuclear force–one of the four basic forces in nature – to bring us together.

Sending out very high-frequency electromagnetic oscillating waves, I finally collided with a heavy element I was suitably matched, whereupon, following the rule of atom-ion interaction, like two nuclei, we fused, amalgamating into a compound, our physical properties dereferenced by introducing ourselves using our names. In spite of the probabilistic qualities of particles, with the wave-particle duality, and doubts over their position and momentum, as they are spread out all over without any specific location, we had found each other. Quantum mechanics, and its uncertainty principle, may not be intuitive to everyone, but it does provide a theoretical basis for the understanding of atomic structure and behaviour, and, by extension, how nature works, as the whole of the universe, within the subatomic world, rests on chance and randomness. The lecture room, a microcosm of real life, while having fostered innumerable communication interaction instances, was now also facilitating their development and proliferation.

After coming into contact and covalently bonding, we now formed a stable molecule. Having reached a crucial temperature, with a chemical change, our transmutation from a physical state to a biological one was precipitating the interactive process, because, however advanced modern technology is nowadays, every experimental scientist knows that many more synaptic connections are possible between two organic cells than between two silicon chips. We were living flesh, not dead matter. We did not merely have a mass and occupy space, we were also alive. In contrast to the previous intense neutron bombardment and agitation, the hall was now a quiet, low-level radiation environment, with only minute traces of alpha and beta particles, and gamma rays emitting from natural sources – normal background radiation. Ionising emission surrounds us at all times.

It had become the laboratory where our polymerisation had been the catalyst of a self-sustaining general osmotic reaction. Membranous, cytoplasmic, mitochondrial binary items were widely scattered; everyone was exchanging ideas. We now coexisted in complete symbiosis, feeding on each other with enzymatic enthusiasm. Food for thought to satisfy our appetite for information and hunger to learn, nourishment to our souls, and spiritual nutrition to boost our minds' metabolism of knowledge. Hopefully, the chemistry would continue working, with more successful collisions producing enough activation energy at the moment of impact to induce further syntheses, the formation of new bonds with others creating even greater synergy. Energy is involved whenever a change of any sort occurs – energy being the ability to create change – and, fortuitously, there was an abundance of energy in the room. Therefore, I was convinced additional change would come about, and many more great things would happen.

I asked my companion, Paul, a few questions to which he promptly replied, and then I too gave him some answers. In a course such as this one, we find people with different academic backgrounds. I learned that he was a mature student and had done a few casual jobs before resuming his studies. I myself have had various occupations in diverse places: I have worked as a tour guide, as an interpreter, and as a tutor. I have also worked in factories, on farms, and in restaurants, among other places. I have emptied garbage, swept floors, cleaned toilets. Not the most glamorous of professions, but they certainly provided me with some undoubtedly valuable experiences as I have a holistic approach to life. I even had a military career, albeit an ephemeral one, as I was once drafted to serve. I then discovered there were two kinds of people the army would never accept: those it considered too idiotic and those it considered too clever. Official secrecy forbids me from revealing my classification. I can only say that I found the psychometric tests rather challenging.

After the interviews, and having learned a lot more about our new friends, we were asked to assemble into groups of four and each present a person to the entire cohort of students. Ultimately, as a final task, we designed a sketch of our own choosing depicting a logical analysis of what had occurred that afternoon within the class. We decided to map out our diagram using distinctive computer flow charts and symbols on the white board, all showing our polymorphous structure. The key idea we pointed out was the gradual progression that had taken place from the outset when we were just single, to when we formed a pair, before becoming a cluster of four speaking to the whole gathering of seventy students. We prevailed in several allotropic forms, going over different physical phases. We had started out as generated individual numerals, continued as perceptible bodies, then through metamorphosis, developed into living physiological entities, eventually mutating into real human beings able to communicate. As we initially behaved like particles, we did not know precisely where our partners were. They could almost have been anywhere until we looked for them; that was our reality. Our exact position or state was never certain before a measurement was made. Though difficult to fully comprehend, I attempted to achieve the phenomenon of quantum entanglement, where two particles stay intertwined. If the particles remain close together and their properties become connected, no matter the distance between them afterwards, their fates remain inextricably linked, regardless of how far apart they end up.

Extensive mathematical and scientific rigour had helped me make favourable predictions with no compelling errors, lessening the odds of getting it wrong to infinitesimally small, indeed, taking into account the margin of error, the finding statistically significant. Then, applying multivariate analysis using multiple linear regression, and matrix algebra, among other models, with abstractions in theoretical physics, even experimenting splitting the atom to create a critical mass of repeating exchanges, and a continuous loss and gain of electrons between our chemical species through different redox reactions, we acted both as reducing and oxidising agents. Also, promoting spontaneous exothermic combustions, with high thermal diffusivity and conductivity, greeting and expressing ourselves with great warmth when we met, confident we had long half-lives and would not disintegrate rapidly, all leading to a positive concluding outcome – the oxygen supporting effective communication essential to human life. Furthermore, unlike neutrinos from radioactive decay, which seldom interact with anything else, we were core nuclear material that had established several diversified mutual and reciprocal relationships around ourselves, seemingly stray neutrons from cosmic ray exposure; the constant shelling of the atmosphere. We were *ipso facto* strongly correlated. And so, we actually presented our map in front of our peers, each one of us in turn introducing someone and giving a rather successful interpretation of the day's exciting events. Without any stomach cramps.

SECOND WEEK

We assembled in the hall with a clearer idea of this course and began the study of that day's theme: body language, which plays an important role in communication. A substantial portion of humanity's communication is non-verbal, and non-verbal details reveal who we are and affect how we relate to other people. We were required to form into pairs and ask our partners some questions, observing his or her body language. I interviewed Tony, a very cheerful student who smiled very often. He moves his arms and hands around a lot when he speaks; that gives him the confidence to make a point. He is jovial, and his charm is certainly one of his qualities. He does not think that he has any facial expressions, but a smile is a facial expression. He also said he tends to pull faces when he is lost; I had actually noticed that the other day when he had forgotten how to navigate within the mainframe computer directory structure. And he makes eye contact with the person he is speaking to. He added that he likes his clothes to communicate his consciousness – whatever that means – and that he changes his style of dress frequently, just to be different. He admitted that he was an extrovert, a statement I would not contradict, looking at his flashy pair of jeans with white and blue stripes. In his opinion, clothes are very important in communication and at work. For that reason, he is very fashion-conscious. Body language is for Tony an effective communication method, and he likes to think he communicates his personality through body language.

I was interviewed also, but my opinion differed as I do not really pay much attention to bodies and I have little interest in clothes. I am more interested in the actual personality and qualities of a person rather than in his or her clothing. I concern myself with the substance of the person and not the superficial details like dress code, giving more relevance to the verb 'to be' than to the verbs 'to appear' and 'to pretend'. 'To be or not to be', that is the important question. For me, only the substance matters. *Esse quam videri.* I have found from personal experience that the more useless the person is the more pretentious they are. Are the most ignorant usually not the most arrogant? In any case, I, for one, habitually dress anyhow, wearing the first shirt I set my hands on in the morning. It is true that very often I look like a tramp, but I just cannot be bothered with my presentation, which reflects my bohemian and nomadic temperament. As far as I am concerned, my personal sartorial opinion is that clothes are more important to keep me warm than to communicate.

I know that in our society, there is an emphasis on the image we project. A formal suit is *de rigueur* for men and if one is not wearing any, one is not to be taken seriously. But does that mean one is worthless? Are clothes an accurate enough criterion by which to judge a person? I do not believe so. Besides, appearances are very often deceptive. I hear a lot of fuss about the importance of clothes at work. This may be justified to a certain extent, but it should not be generalised, because corporate image and competence are two different things. It might be helpful for an encyclopaedia salesman to look like a penguin, but that does not bring any advantage to a technician. If one is, say, involved in programming, wearing a beautiful tie will not make any difference to the final result. I tried it once, yet my program did not compile any faster. Though I admit that body language, which is also about expressions, emotions, and reactions, can certainly be useful in certain circumstances. I recall a personal experience while making a trip in a remote region of Asia where I did not speak nor understand the local dialect. I then realised a smile could work wonders when I needed information or had to buy some food – a smiling face transcended all language barriers. Communicating without talking, that is non-verbal communication.

On this subject, our senses are very important. For instance, smell as a form of communication is older than the human race and more basic than language, and it is the most faithful of all the senses in terms of memory. It is our first means of tuning into the world; newborn babies recognise their mothers by their scent long before their eyes can focus on their face. Smell is the most evocative of all bodily faculties, as it relates to mood, memory, and image. The weakest waft of perfume can bring back nostalgic thoughts and have a profound effect on our temper of the moment. Psychological tests have shown that scents increase the wearer's productivity at work and their general sense of well-being. When an office was scented with lemon, keyboard operators reported a 50 per cent reduction in errors. These studies also revealed that fragrance significantly improved the state of mind and largely eased feelings such as stress, nervousness, animosity, and lethargy. In Mediterranean countries and in the Orient, the burning of incense is not only confined to religious ceremonies and warding off evil spirits – purifying the surroundings – but also performed to make the conditions in a room or a location more agreeable with a pleasing odour.

For centuries it has been accepted that aromas are the key to amorous conquest. The limbic system, the body's central control for emotion, mood, motivation, and sexual behaviour, part of the brain structure, can be stimulated by smell. Love is after all a chemical process and lovers often claim that they feel as if they are literally flooded by chemicals. A meeting of eyes, a movement of lips, a touch of hands, or a whiff of scent, can all start off a tide, beginning in the brain and rushing along the nerves through the blood. And in the brain, neurons communicate through chemicals called neurotransmitters, molecules that seep out of one neuron and excite another, triggering electrical signals that produce thoughts, emotions, memories, and desires. One property of perfume has to do with image. It says a great deal about us, and I have heard of people who choose fragrances to convey to others their true personality. It is, for some, vital to the way they see themselves and the way they want others to see them. Humans can recognise thousands of different odours detected by olfactory receptor neurones in the nose. As smell is the only sense with direct connection to the brain, scent is the most direct and profound impression we can have of a person.

Communicating through touch is another important non-verbal behaviour, having the power to reach parts that are often beyond speaking, with enormously powerful emotional significance. If someone is sad or in pain, taking hold of their hand or putting an arm around their shoulder is often much more effective than words. Touch is probably one of the most efficient forms of communication from the moment humans are born. There has been substantial research on the importance of touch in infancy and early childhood, with parents instinctively beginning to gently cuddle and caress their newborn baby, where tactile stimulation facilitates emotional growth and attachment between both. As the largest organ in the human body, the skin is constantly growing and changing in sensitivity, with sensory receptors picking up enormous quantities of information and sending them to the brain. Touch not only communicates emotions without the need for words, it also creates a sense of closeness and proximity to others; shaking hands, hugging, holding, caressing, or patting on the back, all suggest a feeling of intimacy that can say more than countless well-chosen words.

All successful salespeople are experts in body language. They tend to use eye contact to express sincerity, head nods and tilts to indicate interest, open posture and gestures to show they have nothing to hide, and brief body interaction such as a firm handshake to give the impression of being warm and easy to get on with. The people best at selling can effectively charm their customers by subtly mirroring their body language and way of talking, and by matching the speed of their voices and the rate of their breathing to that of their clients. Therefore, to achieve their goals, top sales people carefully observe their potential buyers; restless feet could be a sign of nervousness and stress, metronomic gestures such as taping a foot or a pen tend to signal impatience – although the seller would certainly not insist too hard at that point – a scratching of the neck may indicate uncertainty and indecision, folded arms would be a defensive intention, and a rubbing of hands could show underlying enthusiasm. Gestures are indeed an important way to communicate meaning without words.

As idioms vary from one nation to the other, body language patterns also change with cultures. What is considered normal and permissible in one society could be taboo in another. People communicate in terms of their own experiences. For instance, in many Middle Eastern and Asian countries, it is customary to freely touch people of the same sex, holding each other's hands and walking arm in arm. These displays are not signs of homosexuality but of friendship and closeness as 'brothers' or 'sisters'. On the other hand, in these cultures, there is no equivalent to the social greeting of hugging and kissing between people of the opposite sex. Physical demonstrations of affection in public between the sexes, even between husband and wife, are frowned upon as they are seen as being too intimate. Consequently, Westerners visiting these places should always aim for the most respectable behaviour and avoid publicly touching, kissing, or hugging people of the opposite sex, as it could be mistaken for signals of amorous interest rather than social friendliness and cause some embarrassment. Another example that springs to mind that highlights potential cultural misunderstandings can be found in Buddhist countries; as the head is the highest part of the body – spiritually as well as literally – it is therefore considered rude to touch another person on the head deliberately. And, conversely, in these locations of the world, the feet are the lowest part of the body, and, as such, one should not point the sole of the foot at anyone, a gesture foreign visitors often do accidentally when they cross their legs.

The purpose of this class was for us to become more aware of non-verbal communication – as we can understand a person better if we are able to interpret his or her body language. Although I do not pay much attention to the impressions people make – or try to make – I agree that observing them is worthwhile. Take Val, the team leader. When she is giving a lecture, she is always smiling and sending out energy, which can be felt in the back of the classroom, contrasting with people like me who perhaps radiate as much charisma as uranium oxide, even though I was told when I was younger that I had the looks of an Italian movie star. Indeed, I remember a few years ago while in India, a country of great culture, civilisation, and history – India is so fascinating because it is like no other country – I was approached to appear in a film as an extra. At that time, I was incredibly photogenic, irresistibly charming, amazingly good-looking and devastatingly attractive – I am not prone to using superlatives lightly. Yes, extraordinarily, I was also classically handsome and elegant. Words such as smart, stylish, dashing, suave, debonair, swashbuckling, and many others – but I shall restrain myself – were all appropriate ways of describing me. Only a genuine sense of modesty prevented me from entering the 'Sexiest Man Alive' contest, which I would have won hands-down anyway.

As a demigod equipped with such fantastic features, I felt that, at the very least, I deserved a supporting role so I declined the offer. Working as a mere extra? Excuse me, I was not that desperate. With hindsight, I realise such an attitude may have cost me a promising career in the movie industry. On another occasion, while on a plane – true story! – I was asked by an air hostess whether I was a film star; I humbly replied that I was, but requested her to please not tell anyone as I was travelling incognito. My answer had an electric effect on her–exactly how many volts I could not say – and she melted. I really thought she was going to faint; I even feared the worst. In those days, I had to be very careful when approaching women, keeping in mind the meaning of the expression 'drop-dead gorgeous', always critically aware of its potentially fatal consequences.

After all, I certainly never wanted to be charged with manslaughter. Yet, since I was *compos mentis*, and though I have the right to remain silent, I admit to pleading guilty to multiple counts of breaking the heart of many a lady, thus causing grievous bodily harm with intent, so there is no presumption of innocence. A crime of passion in the eyes of those concerned, maybe, but, hopefully, not enough to convict me in a court of law, even if there is no statute of limitations. Hence, I have got away with murder.

Although I have not been called to the bar and I cannot pretend to be considered a practising barrister, with a right of audience before all courts, I should be allowed to argue on behalf of myself. Therefore, in my defence, I am entitled to make a plea in mitigation before a jury returns a verdict and any sentence is passed, obtaining the least possible punishment as penalty, evidence of true remorse, and any effort that I, the defendant, attempt to avoid reoffending should be taken into consideration, following this request to be judged with compassion and leniency after pondering my *mea culpa*. While I do not dispute the *mens rea* and *actus reus* of the offence, as they could be proven beyond a reasonable doubt by the prosecution, contrary to common perception, I was not dealt a good hand by fate and I should be viewed as a victim rather than a perpetrator, thus indicted and put on trial with empathy, and then acquitted, or at least discharged, especially since I have no previous convictions or criminal record, setting a precedent as a result, even though the burden of proof that I am of good character is still on me, a probable aggravating factor.

I invoke *force majeure* to clear myself of liability and avoid becoming the focus of a *cause célèbre*. Blessed with a most sensational muscular and athletic body, endowed with the fabulous physical appearance of a male supermodel oozing allure and charisma, one might believe that I have it all. But imagine how being relentlessly and incessantly pursued by members of the opposite sex can be a gruesome and distressing – indeed excruciatingly nightmarish – experience. Impossible to keep the ladies at bay. Disadvantageous circumstances outside my control in life. And, over time, after countless social dates and romantic encounters with numerous sweethearts and *inamoratas*, meeting the most stunning girls of striking beauty with great taste in men, who would be willing to testify under oath as witnesses if subpoenaed – making a sworn declaration and be cross-examined by any lawyer or attorney instituting legal proceedings against me, even signing a notarised affidavit, with no intent of perverting the course of justice and committing perjury. All these women without exception came up with the same question: how could any woman ever possibly resist me? I rest my case.

What a shame that I have lost those phenomenal qualities – almost all my muscles are gone – possibly because of my peripatetic and itinerant lifestyle. Well, at least I am now more mature, and thankfully, no one chases me any longer. When I take off my T-shirt on a crowded beach, I need not fear of being mobbed by overexcited female fans, with the riot police having to be called to rescue and protect me, before restoring and maintaining order, as would have been required earlier. I therefore lead a relatively normal and peaceful life. Nevertheless, I understand that without doubt body language can be very purposeful in different situations: many use scent to cultivate the art of seduction, or gesture and nod their heads to convince. Others pull faces to entertain and to amuse, while some use their fingers to count, or sign language to communicate. And I do not mention those who want to be dressed to kill.

THIRD WEEK

After a recess week, we began this Monday afternoon with a review of the topics studied so far, before progressing to written communication. We were given handouts describing body language and communication in more detail. Fundamentally, communication is a process which transfers a meaningful message from point A to point B. Communication is the transmission of information from one person to another. This procedure comprises several elements, such as the sender, the message, the medium, and the receiver, and can have different characteristics depending on the form of communication. Civilisation is made possible by communication in its various forms. The level of communication distinguishes humankind from animals and differentiates modern communities from primitive ones. Communication is the lifeblood of a society.

Intrapersonal communication is the most familiar as it is the one done with oneself while thinking, which is something I do very often. The interpersonal type involves communication between a certain number of people, whereas extrapersonal communication applies to machines. Why do we communicate? Along with eating and sleeping, communication is probably the most basic need of the human species, so we communicate to satisfy personal needs: to establish relationships, to learn about things, people, or places, to entertain, and more. We certainly take better notice of communication if it is relevant to our interests and requirements, or confirms attitudes and beliefs already held. One example demonstrates how important expression is to a society: in the eighteenth century, the newly created United States of America included freedom of speech as the First Amendment of its Constitution.

On the hand-out, there was also a paragraph on the importance of the self. We live in an environment that influences our nature. Past experiences, previous successes or failures, personality, and culture all have an effect on the way we interact. We all have a self-image which is somewhat formed by how other people see us and react to us. We are here indeed touching the domain of psychology; I was not wrong when I said earlier that communication was a vast area. Here were answers to some of the questions I had in mind at the beginning. We were now in our third week and I was getting a clearer grasp of this subject.

We explored written communication through some simple exercises consisting of various sentences; they were in different tones and we had to describe them. In the process, we were given some vocabulary to add to our repertoire. Words like peremptory, pedantic, derogatory, subservient, reprimand, patronise, and many more were mentioned. During the lecture, emphasis was put on the style and tone of the business letter. Indeed, writing a letter conveys an image of a business – just as body language communicates an image of a person. The tone used also makes an impression that can be interpreted, so tact is needed in business correspondence to avoid any unwanted complications. Presentation is also important; a letter written on recycled paper would have a different impact from one written on pure white stationery.

In the second half of the lecture, we were given a couple of business letters to analyse and reformat. These letters dealt with customer relations. The first was a reply to a person who had sent her computer for repairs and apparently had received no news. In it, the company stated bluntly that for her to be calling them every day was pointless. She was advised to get in touch with the particular store from which she had purchased the device, because the head office did not know anything about the transaction. From the tone of this reply, we infer that the company lacked coordination and was unhelpful when it came to solving customers' problems. For a firm dealing in computers, they are not serious and professional. They might as well be selling oranges and bananas.

The second letter was a response to a query from a client who had not received her goods; the department manager derogated on his responsibilities by stating, simply, that the client should make some inquiries at the local post office. Then he moved on to a different subject with a lot of unnecessary disclosures about the finances of his company.

These were examples of badly written letters to avoid at all costs. Again, the tone of a business letter is critical as it can affect the relationship with customers. We have to put ourselves on the receiving end to realise what consequences letters written in such a manner can have. We need to appear educated – even if we are not. As business executives, we have to keep one paramount notion in mind: it is our customers that make our business – any business for that matter. Without them we lose our *raison d'être*. The customers are always right, and even if they are not, and occasionally a nuisance, we should try to accommodate them. This may seem trivial, but it is a fundamental aspect of business management.

Writing is probably the most powerful form of communication and certainly the most indelible, immune to the passage of time. Who remembers the exact content of a conversation or a telephone call after a few days? Whereas we are still able to read the thoughts of writers who lived thousands of years ago – writers never die. Writing is also possibly the method of communication that allows the most freedom, the least prone to censorship. One can be muzzled, telephone lines can be disconnected, radio transmissions can be scrambled, but it is virtually impossible to be prevented from writing. A past recipient of the Nobel Prize in Literature, Wole Soyinka, was once a political prisoner in his country, but he continued to write poems and essays on toilet roll in his cell – the creative mind cannot be imprisoned. Another Nobel laureate, Aleksandr Solzhenitsyn, experienced the brutal conditions and horrors of the Soviet gulag system but still managed to become an influential literary figure and a powerful voice against totalitarianism, oppression and injustice. Even the most autocratic regimes never succeed in uprooting underground publications.

Writing is mental gymnastics calling for a synchronised use of all muscular partitions of the brain, as it is simultaneously a creative, linguistic, and logical effort. No other exercise is capable of stretching the mind as much. A most competitive sport having many aficionados trying to improve their personal best, and requiring, for spiritual athletes aspiring to be champions, sound intellectual fitness, with rigorous literary workout plans of long hours of training doing the heavy lifting, preferably on bars–or rather on nerves – of steel. *Mens sana in corpore sano.* Poetry in motion. A healthy body fosters a sharp mind.

Since ancient days, writers have played a significant role within their societies. Today, in many countries, writers are still idolised and epitomised, perceived as spokespersons reporting the words of those who do not have access to expression, and can subsequently place themselves at the service of a cause or a community. Writers are witnesses of their time, and the zeitgeist they produce is their spiritual testimony. As we are required to assess our strengths and weaknesses in the course, I can certainly say that I am more comfortable in front of a sheet of paper than in front of an audience. I suppose I have some innate abilities to express myself in writing, and I continue developing my proficiency because that is not an end in itself. As well as strong analytical and problem-solving skills, good writers also need a talent for innovative thinking and organisational aptitudes for structuring their ideas; they should think differently and from a new perspective. Writers must be able to think outside the box. Therefore, I believe that with written words I can have more impact and reach a wider public than with spoken ones. I can voice my opinions louder with a pen than with any microphone.

FOURTH WEEK

The auditorium was half empty at the start of this afternoon. Had there been a massive dropout in our course? Or was the approaching deadline for the maths assignment causing much anguish in some of my peers? Nevertheless, it was with a certain agitation that Mike walked in to commence the lecture. Being the only male in the team, he executes his style with the composure of a gentleman, remaining unruffled and always in control. With him, we proceeded with the study of the written report, a complement to last week's topic.

Report writing has its rules, the first of which – and probably the most important - is to have a structure and a good plan of action. The structure and plan will guide us, making our work and research easier. As an exercise, we were asked to decide on a report format by composing draft headings and subheadings. The specification of the report was that our course director had asked us to investigate students' reactions to the availability and efficiency of computer provision at the university, and we had to make some recommendations. I teamed up with John to do this exercise. We decided that for an introduction, we would write a summary pointing out the purpose of the report, an analysis of hardware and software resources useful to students. We suggested having a main heading for each department, in which we would have a subheading describing the available technical items. And in another section, we would specify access time and training facilities before the conclusion, where we would disclose our observations and recommendations. Having this pattern would then make our investigations much easier.

In the second part of this lecture, we were given some important notions on report writing by Anna and Chris. A report is a formal presentation of information given by one party to another. A report is based on facts; it is a means of communicating knowledge or advice from the sender, who has collected and structured the evidence, to the receiver who has asked for the report for a particular purpose. And we were told that reports can be classified into routine reports, information reports, investigative reports, project reports, and technical reports. A report usually consists of three sections: an introduction, a body, and a conclusion. And, it should have a title and indicate a reference – the person reading it could be different from the one who actually requested it.

The report is of great importance in business, where decisions always have to be made on the basis of information, the clarity of which affects the quality of the decisions made. These facts have to be presented to the decision makers in a clear, concise, and precise form – the advantages of the written report. Each type of report presents its own challenge, but all must adhere to one principle: the needs of the reader are all-important, and the material must be clearly and logically organised. If a report does not serve the reader, it will not be effective. Someone may create excellent, original work, but if the presentation, writing, and layout of the report do not equal the quality of the content, reader goodwill is lost, and the report itself may be ignored or its author's technical competence, often unjustly, called into question. It could be added that the higher we communicate within the hierarchy, the more concise the report should be, as time is a valuable commodity to management. In whatever position we shall work, and in whatever industry or organisation, we will most certainly have to produce reports; therefore we should be *au fait* with report writing.

Both lecturers are involved in writing; Anna told us she had been doing it for the past twenty-five years. She gave us a tip to avoid writer's block: aim to write badly and edit well. I personally agree with this, as I find editing to be the most important but also the most difficult and time-consuming part in writing. Fortunately, the advent of micro-computerisation years ago was the *deus ex machina* set to alleviate this burden. If the machine was the computer, the god was the word processor which henceforth blessed writers with absolute control over their work. A divine tool worshipped by some with an almost religious fervour, a ritual often producing the most heavenly results, and even performing, in moments of poetic licence, perhaps a sign from a deity, miracles enshrined in the holy grail of one's prose written with biblical cadence – an offering of grateful homage and thanksgiving in words as praise to such almighty creation. Though not gospel truth, this benediction is certainly a revelation, possibly the answer to many an author's prayers, lifting their spirit after much soul-searching and display of sacred devotion with pastoral equanimity, helping members of this large lettered congregation find salvation by writing with profound evangelical imagination, while providing them with angelic guidance to reach the promised land during the course of literate pilgrimages made by such disciples of so venerated a doctrine – an epiphany as the homily goes.

A software of cardinal significance, elevating the few who have enough faith in their scriptural abilities – devout believers in their creative potential, respecting the highest celestial standards, and applying the most ecclesiastical rigour, with a little providential inspiration – to literary sainthood above the ranks of mere mortals, raising the individuals so honoured as icons of heroic reverence – a consecration. Solemn confirmation such rite is administered to those able to achieve full communion within their sacramental character, a means of receiving sanctifying grace. And while I am not preaching only to the converted, and may pontificate with missionary zeal, giving a sermon construed as a crusade in favour of a sacrilegious cause going against canonical works, sounding like a prophet with a messianic vision of artistic redemption, proclaiming an unorthodox expectation of symbolic universal cultural resurrection, I have no intention of opposing any particular dogma – I am just the messenger. A scholarly apostle, advocating a reformation of how writing is done, even though that can still be a matter of debate. And, if that seems heretical to some, there is no need to conduct an inquisition and crucify me, burning me at the stake; I repent, asking for forgiveness and seeking absolution, hoping I am spared the ordeal of an *auto-da-fé* and not forced to confess my sins and publicly recant my views – or have to submit to any other penance as a form of atonement until judgement day. Amen.

I like to compare the art of writing to sculpture. Just as a sculptor first cuts a piece of wood of a basic shape, then painstakingly carves and smoothes out the details before applying the final polish, the writer first jots down ideas on paper, shapes them, modifies them, then patiently puts the finishing touches before obtaining a masterpiece – a *tour de force* involving precision work. Good writing is fine craftsmanship. And as with any art, writing requires determination, perseverance, and a lot of practice. I also once overheard a female friend saying that writing was like giving birth. I cannot possibly know, but I indeed sometimes find the procedure rather painful.

Mastering the craft of writing is a long process of trial and error. The best way to teach oneself effective writing is to write. My *modus operandi* in writing is always to keep on writing. It is no use talking, discussing, debating, or arguing about it. Only by constant and regular proactive writing does one become a more proficient writer. My adopted pedagogical methodology is constructivism – learning by doing. A *sine qua non* for achieving excellence in this field is hard work. And, like the garbage man, the man – or woman – of letters should not be afraid to roll in the mud as writing is a dirty business. Compared to real writers, politicians are just innocent school children.

Having writing skills is very useful in virtually any field. Even in a fundamental subject such as mathematics it is essential. In the coursework I mentioned earlier, explanations – or the ability to write clearly and accurately – accounted for 20 per cent of the overall mark. In computer programming, which is not only about code, being able to write plain English is invaluable, if only to produce proper documentation. And even those involved in purely scientific research need to communicate the results of their work to their colleagues in a written form.

Like great cuisine, great literature is able to lift the spirit and inspire and feed the mind. Just as good cookery is produced by the most proficient chefs using exclusively a range of quality ingredients, the best writers are master chefs selecting only an excellent mix of appetizing words carefully chosen from the *crème de la crème* of nouns, verbs, and adjectives, among other fine culinary products, harnessing all the experience and devotion they can muster to concoct as starters on the elaborate entertaining menu, palatable *hors-d'oeuvre* cocktails of varied phrases and sentences to stimulate a desire for more, followed by the most delectable *pièces de résistance* marinated in delicious beautiful prose, composed from original personal recipes, spiced with hot passionate condiments exuding powerful aromas of evocative ideas stewed in innovative dishes, adding extra sauce of succulent textual effects and exquisite figures of speech for enhanced flavour and piquancy, delicately prepared alongside fresh savoury linguistic salads artistically decorated, creatively seasoned, and peppered with a blend of delightful allegorical dressings, including a dash of onomatopoeic salt, and a *soupçon* of zestful rhetorical relish. Plus generous assortments of rich, sweet, bright, dazzling, mouth-watering metaphors, blazing alight over the pages, sparking the imagination while igniting strong emotions, fanning the flames of intellectual illumination, finally complementing the special main courses as classic *flambé* desserts setting the world on fire and leaving a pleasant long-lasting aftertaste – all readily served alfresco in print to be avidly devoured by hungry readers eager to satisfy their craving for literary comfort food – a feast for the most discerning gastronomy lovers.

In the final part of this session, we were sent to the library to find some materials for our video presentation. Yes, the presentation was in less than three weeks, and I had deliberately forgotten about this task, expecting it to disappear. I was not the only one though, because when I questioned my partner as to whether he had written any comments so far, he simply answered that he had just been thinking about it. Well, I suggested it would then be better to start giving concrete expression to our cogitative work on paper. For this class assignment, we had a choice of five topics, and it had to be done in pairs, so I teamed up with Jonas. At first, he proposed we choose the option on the social cost of introducing new technology, but being the practical person that I am, I quickly pointed out that this involved too much research and study of facts. It would thus be wiser to select an easier and simpler theme for discussion: a career in computing. As presenting a video was difficult and stressful enough, it was better to tackle a more obvious and straightforward subject, *faute de mieux*.

The university library is a gigantic database in itself. How can one retrieve the relevant documentation for a project? I proceeded in the most straightforward way by keying in 'career in computing' on the computer index catalogue and the screen presented me with titles on careers in computing and information technology. Amazing information technology. The widespread use of this technology, providing large amount of digital information that can effectively be harnessed, is affecting virtually every area of society, and while doing so, empowering, enriching, and enlightening mankind. The frontiers of computers are boundless and seem to offer limitless potential. In any case, finding a book in a fraction of a second among thousands of volumes could only be possible with such technology. There was a time, not so long ago, when one needed a book in a library one had to look through countless numbers of shelves, and further there was no guarantee of locating it. However, nowadays, the computer performs the search for us. It is said that there is no stopping progress, so when can we expect a computer to read a book for us?

FIFTH WEEK

On this rainy autumn afternoon, we received some precise indications on the presentation assignment to be held in a fortnight. A list was read out with the exact time and location for each group. We were required to arrive at the beginning of the hour slot in which we were to perform, lest we disturb those currently presenting. We got together in pairs to continue working on this task. I was working with Jonas, an intelligent fellow student who manifestly had an aptitude for public speaking. We consulted our documentation before drafting a structure for our talk. It would be conventional, with an introduction, a main body, and a conclusion. We shared the parts we would present, keeping in mind that only ten minutes were allocated – a short time indeed to treat such a wide topic. It was decided that in the introduction, we would outline the role of computers in general, and in the main part, in the first section, we would highlight some careers available in computing, before describing in detail one particular job, with a conclusion at the end.

We had a word with Chris, one of the lecturers, who suggested we could speak about stereotypes in the computer world. We learned that although she had no technical knowledge of programming, she had designed a best-selling educational computer game for children – a fact that proves creative people can also play a role in computing. It is true that very often we associate computers with dry technicians, but nowadays we are finding more and more people with different backgrounds in this field as computers are becoming increasingly popular. Now, they are used to compose music, to design graphics, as well as to process photographic pictures. Recently, I was reading a review about a software package which allowed the artist to paint on the screen like he or she would on a canvas, using various shades of colours which could be modified or erased instantly at will. Looking at the published photos, the outcome was undoubtedly outstanding. Computers are also ideal for implementing multimedia – the combination of modes of communication such as video, audio, and text. As computers are more than a new technology, crucially, they are a means of enhancing human creativity, the future should be very exciting.

Another area where computers play a major role is in artificial intelligence. There are different categories of artificial intelligence software: expert, or knowledge-based, systems apply reasoning capabilities to problems in order to reach a conclusion or recommendation; intelligent agents, adaptive systems working independently to execute specific repetitive or predictive computer-related tasks. And generic algorithms, able to generate increasingly optimum solutions to questions by providing various answers from which the best are selected and used again to produce even better results, are designed on optimisation techniques based on the concepts of natural evolution – finding the combination of inputs giving the best outputs. Arguably, the most significant attempt at the creation of artificial intelligence has used the pattern of the brain as the template for a rather complicated computer architecture. Neural networks comprise linked microprocessors emulating the complex mesh of interconnected neurons within the brain, a multitude of processors – nodes where data is processed – joined through communication circuits. Neural computers learn by example as they are not programmed like ordinary computers; they not only execute a set of instructions but also incorporate feedback where the output of a node can be returned as input to another for self-correction, consequently achieving better communication and comprehension of their domain and environment. There is, however, still much contention about whether computers will ever be able to think or display the traits normally considered essential for intelligence. Personally, I very much doubt it. I may only start believing it when I see a machine pass the ultimate test: writing a book on its own. The words of John F. Kennedy still resonate after many decades, and they certainly will continue to do so in the future: 'Man is still the most extraordinary computer of all.' Nevertheless, while the debate continues, research into artificial intelligence is bringing a better understanding of human brain function and intelligence.

In this first half of the session, we had the honour of having a professional actor give us some theatrical techniques. And who could be better qualified than an actress to teach us some stage secrets? She mentioned a few rules to help smoothen our performances, the most important of which was to rehearse, rehearse, and rehearse. In so doing, we would be able to master and be in control of the situation. We should be able to cope with any eventualities, as the main reason people worry about speaking publicly is the fear of the unforeseen event that can happen suddenly. To be prepared, we therefore have to practise, and she emphasised that rehearsal was the key to this. It has to be done as much as possible, in any spare moment: between two classes, on the bus, in the bathroom, in bed, well...? That is apparently how professional actors work.

Another tip was to take our time; we should not rush a discussion as no one would understand. The point is to *communicate* with the audience; if this goal is not achieved, then the delivery is a failure. Walking tall was another rule; we need to show spectators that we have confidence in ourselves; though this is not easy, it comes with practice. A smile is also very useful as it puts everyone at ease. One more piece of advice was to know our stage, the room we will be in, and the equipment we shall use. She explained a breathing technique to relax us: we should pause, breath through the nose, and then through the mouth – that is supposed to calm us. In order to avoid direct eye contact with those in attendance and becoming distracted, we should look about six inches above their heads, while still giving the impression we are looking at them. One final hint was to be enthusiastic about our activity, which made me wonder how one can possibly be enthusiastic about a presentation.

After her lecture, we assembled in groups of ten students and started our rehearsals. Each one of us stood up and gave a little exhibition of our work so far, within the little groups. This series of mini-stagings was actually not so bad. I think we did not have enough confidence in ourselves, which is why we were afraid of this experience. I was certainly right in thinking that this video assignment was making us dither. Its purpose was to give us practice so that when it came to the real world, where we would not be allowed to make any mistakes, we would be prepared. I just hope that in that world I will not be forced to make too many public speaking appearances given my *parti pris*.

In the second part of the session, we were handed general guidelines on public discourses with a few examples. Some were obvious, others not. We were told that when doing a talk, we must think about our audience. We should undertake some research, draft a structure with an introduction, a main body, and a conclusion. We also have to appear self-confident and in control. And we need to speak clearly and fluently, and be aware of onlookers' body language, which can reveal how attentive they are. In contrast to the past couple of lectures, this day's class centred on the verbal forms of communication that required particular skills altogether different from those necessary in writing. Performing in front of a public gathering is a talent one either has or one has not – and I have not. But then I cannot have everything.

SIXTH WEEK

I was feeling rather tired and sluggish today, heavy, as if I weighed a ton. This was probably caused by the greasy take-away meal, full of saturated fat, I had had earlier; my digestive system having been unable to cope, and a possible case of indigestion. Or was it my liver? All this junk food is bound to upset my body at some point. I should be more health-conscious and careful with my diet in the future. And, I was still lost in my gastrohepatic thoughts when we began the class with an exercise on note taking in which we were expected to take some notes relevant to the text read out by Anna. But after a few minutes most of us gave up writing, as we were unable to keep up with the reader's pace. The text was about technical communication and documentation, dealing with user manual contents.

Identifying the main ideas was something easier said than done, as we needed practice to be able to write down the major points while listening without missing any of them. After this experience, we understood that taking notes was not so simple; it was an aptitude requiring training.

We were then given a copy of the document and asked to extract the main points from it. The technique in such a case is to single out what is called a topic or a thesis sentence – one that encapsulates the whole text; then we have to summarise in our own words the substantial ideas in each paragraph.

A hand-out was distributed giving us more notions on this form of communication. When we take notes we need to determine a purpose. What kind of records are they? Are they lecture scripts? Are they taken on behalf of someone else? The layout is important; a schematic one can help better our understanding. So can the use of headings and subheadings, or leaving gaps between sections of entries, which makes them easier to read. In writing notes, there are some significant rules to respect: we should read the material carefully, reference the source, *exempli gratia* the author, the book, the date… We should also use our own words, except when quoting directly from the text. It is worth remembering that we are only interested in the essential ideas; any annotations that are ours should be clearly identified. Good notetaking is an exercise that forces us to restructure received information and interpret it in our own way – a useful skill for anyone to have.

Most students find it difficult to take effective notes during lectures; a few hints can help us make the most of these periods. It is necessary to arrive on time with a notepad and a pen, sit where we obtain a good view of the board or overhead projector screen and listen attentively to avoid switching off or allowing our attention to wander. We also need to be aware of both kinds of structures used by lecturers to teach a class. With an expositional format, information is imparted in a logical sequence with factual data; in our jottings we should ensure that we set down the meaningful points and examples in sufficient detail. However, with an argumentative structure, both sides of an argument, case, or discussion are presented; we must therefore express in a concise form the different perspectives and record the outcome or conclusion. Lastly, it should be mentioned that our summaries will form the basis of revision for examinations, and they should therefore be accurate and legible.

Anna outlined five key points in taking notes from speakers. First, we should never give up; which was precisely what our class did at the beginning. We need to pay attention to words that are repeated and copy them down. We should also watch and listen to the presenter as carefully as possible, because his or her attitude – body language for instance – can help us comprehend him or her better. The annotations should be read immediately after the speechmaker has finished so that we have a chance to write anything still present in our minds. Finally, she emphasised the first point again: never give up.

To conclude this first part of the session, Chris showed us a different way to take notes: using a spider diagram. Though it might not suit everyone, it offered an alternative to those familiar with flow charts. This advice made us aware of a prominent skill we need to use in most, if not all, subjects, where the ability to synthesise data and ideas clearly and accurately is essential for a better assimilation. I have been writing notes since my early school days and I continue to do so. Good notetaking is not always straightforward and can be difficult to master, but, as with most things, the solution is to practise. And with a suitable methodology, we can disprove a certain definition of a lecture I once overheard: a transfer of information from the lecturer's notes to the student's without going through either brain.

In the second half of today's period, the progress of our logbook was assessed by a lecturer. One of our assignments was to keep a communication file, which was to be handed in at the end of the semester. This is a personal account containing a good balance of descriptions and analysis of the various activities participated in during this communication module. I believe that developing a critical mind is not only very important in communication, but also in all subjects. Without falling into obsessional scepticism, I do not take anything for granted and try to sift all the information I receive. Whenever I am confronted with an event – and I have come across many in my young life – I always ask myself various questions in order to get a better grasp of it. What is behind it? How good is it? What is the relation of cause and effect? And besides, remarkably, the mind is truly amazing, having unlimited potential. Indeed, the human spirit can overcome the greatest adversity, transcending the most difficult challenges and obstacles, to climb the highest mountains of life and conquer the wildest dreams. There is nothing we cannot achieve when we put our mind to it. That is the triumph of the indomitable human spirit. I am just mentioning this *en passant*.

An intellectually coherent analysis of most situations in life not only gives us a better perspective of potential problems but also avoids deceptions and manipulations because no one holds the monopoly of universal truth – not even the university. As the philosopher René Descartes wrote: 'Nothing is certain, all knowledge must begin with doubt and proceed to the accumulation of a body of evidence before any certainty can be obtained. Nothing may be taken for granted, not even personal existence.' Everything is open to doubt except one's own conscious experience: *cogito, ergo sum* – I think, therefore I am. Mind and matter are separate though interacting. It is our ability to think that proves our actual existence. And I would add this quote from Mahatma Gandhi: 'Persistent questioning and healthy inquisitiveness are the first requisite for acquiring learning of any kind.' The same person who said: 'Live as if you were to die tomorrow. Learn as if you were to live forever.' With Albert Einstein also stating: 'The important thing is not to stop questioning.' A sound critical mind is certainly invaluable to assimilate proper knowledge and education.

This logbook is a personal outlook on the communication course, reflecting how we perceived, felt, and interpreted it. But it is also a reflection on life and the world in general. The result, this actual volume, is my *weltanschauung*. I had so far written a few hundred words for each session and this was my first draft. I had at least the main concepts and ideas on paper, they just needed to be developed further with additional remarks and editing. Chris reviewed the work I had already done, and she said she was really impressed with my choice of metaphors. I simply replied, with all the humility appropriate in such circumstances, that I was just an aspiring writer hoping to make it in the literary world, a jungle where, using a pen as a machete, only the most creative survive.

Writing a document such as this one is obviously a very laborious task that should be done gradually and regularly. As we were given *carte blanche* to complete this assignment, my approach was to write down notes after each class, trying not to omit any important detail and making observations while my memory was still fresh, using them as *aides-memoir*. I also used this opportunity to challenge my assumptions and push the boundaries of my understanding, asking thoughtful questions, seeking out diverse viewpoints, engaging in thought experiments, all while reflecting on my thinking processes. I like to think of the finished work as the written justification of my thoughts, beliefs, and character – an *apologia pro vita sua*. And throughout the course, I made sure I set myself weekly objectives. Abiding by such a discipline was not so easy, as I noticed more than a few students who had no notes and were trying to remember what had been done in three previous sessions. Unlike some, I do not subscribe to the theory that keeping a detailed and accurate account of one's activities is a simple and casual affair. Because like all theories, I find it highly theoretical.

SEVENTH WEEK

Today was a special – should I say dreadful – day for those of us who were to give our presentations, something we wanted to be finished with. I had a look at the location in which we would perform later in the afternoon and met others doing last-minute preparation – the atmosphere was perceptibly tense. Jonas and I used an empty classroom to do some final rehearsals before the real one, still trying to keep the length of our talk within the specified time. We needed to be very concise as our chosen topic was extensive. Jonas's part was particularly long as he would be doing the introduction, speaking generally about the available computer careers, the different sectors of the industry, the opportunities, the salaries, and the required qualifications. To illustrate all these points, he would also use a few charts and diagrams.

In my bit, I would give a detailed description of one particular profession: the systems analyst – who many people in the computing industry say has the most interesting and responsible job. And this work is usually done in three phases. First, it involves a careful examination of the needs of a firm or department, and an assessment of how these are currently met. The next stage is to design a suitable system to meet the present and likely future requirements most effectively. And lastly, the systems analyst will probably have to supervise the introduction of the new system if management agrees to go ahead with it.

For a given task, the systems analyst, who must have a deep and wide knowledge and experience of the industry, starts with a feasibility study – a detailed inspection of the work currently performed and the method by which it is done. For that, the analyst must talk to users, perhaps even to customers – possibly to anyone who has a stake in the project – to identify what they need and want from any new system. Here, the important activity is gathering clearly defined business requirements; the focus is on an understanding of the full business functionality of the computer system. This essential part of the job, the investigation and reporting of initial facts, not only requires the ability to get on well with people but also the capacity to sense end users' thoughts, opinions, and concerns clearly good communication skills.

When the evidence has been collected, the next step is to evaluate the situation, usually done by setting out the findings in a flow chart form. Once it is agreed what information will be coming in and what output will be expected, the analyst will define the system – the process to do the job. At this point, he or she looks at different approaches to meeting the requests found, with various solutions compared to determine the best. Many questions are asked. What are the computing needs? What programs should be used? How should the computers be connected? Are there any particular constraints? What are the costs involved? If no current software fits the user's requisites fully, the analyst will call in one or more programmers. When the system to be implemented is brought in and the software approved, the analyst must schedule its introduction, working closely with all the people concerned with the application, and prepare detailed technical documentation. During the actual implementation, the systems analyst will be expected to deal with any matter that may arise, to train the users, and possibly to run the system for a specific period of time.

Our presentation started fairly well with Jonas explaining the different possible professions and showing his charts, but he lost track of the time as he laboured on too many details. Had he forgotten that I was to present the second part? I would not have minded though if he wanted to do the whole talk. Although he had told me he was scared, he looked very confident, and I did not dare interrupt him, but we were running out of time. He finally handed over to me, and I then said my part trying to be as articulate as I could. My explanations were clear but I had to stop before ending the conclusion, as our allotted time was over. I stumbled on a question from the audience, but Jonas masterfully came to my assistance and completed my answer.

After our speech, Jonas admitted he had not realised he had spoken for so long; timing ourselves had indeed been one of the difficulties we encountered during our rehearsals – we wanted to say too much in too little time. We hopped to the library to have a preview of ourselves; it does make quite an impression to view oneself on a screen. It gives us an idea of how other people see us, and nothing escapes the scrutiny of the camera, which records all details, especially body language. Our delivery was good; in fact, we performed with aplomb and great *élan*, conveying an interesting oral display. This assignment was a new experience for me, albeit an anxious one. Though I really did deliver the presentation with complete *sangfroid*, I will not go as far as to say that I did it intentionally and in cold blood without emotion, but at least my blood was certainly not running cold – nor did it make my blood boil. It was nevertheless interesting, as, in the course of its preparation, I learned so much about computer careers in general and systems analysis in particular. Yet, I would not like to be delivering this sort of presentation too often, as I am not terribly keen on public speaking.

I am specifically interested in computer programming and software development, for I believe it is in this field that

I can make the best use of my abilities. Though I might also consider doing some systems analysis when I have more work experience, because it seems an exciting and varied activity, where one sees and learns a lot. Actually, my initial professional ambition was not in computing but civil aviation. I have indeed always wanted to climb on board the left-hand cockpit seat as captain and pilot-in-command of a jumbo jet. Unfortunately, I have not been able to accomplish this goal. Therefore, in the meantime, it looks like I will have to content myself with being just a writer. Life can be harsh for some. And as for Jonas, if he does not find any satisfaction in a computing career, he could always become a politician. Or something like that.

EIGHTH WEEK

As some presentations were still staged, we did not have any formal lecture today, but we had been given a group project a couple of weeks ago and were expected to start working on it. For this, we formed teams of five students to research one of the listed topics, and produce a report outlining our findings, conclusions, and recommendations. Each member was to be allocated a task, with one also nominated to the position of leader, responsible for the completion of the work on time. This exercise was designed to give us group skills practice such as decision making, motivation, and organisation.

We also had to keep a minimum cohesion among ourselves as there was a penalty of fifteen marks if our party was to disband after its formation. We thus needed to forge an *esprit de corps* – easier said than done. Personally, I do not like group work, but I understand that later we will be expected to work with other people, and therefore we should have the ability to be part of a team. With a group undertaking, everyone's contribution is important; so if one fails to deliver, the entire project can collapse as deadlines are not met. And the more people in a meeting, the more possible suggestions are available, and the more difficult it is to find a consensus. Communication therefore lies at the heart of teamwork.

Jonas and I agreed to stay together – why change a working partnership? We were looking for more companions when we met another classmate who needed a group. Being unsupervised, we had to avoid drifting into a gentle state of lethargy, leading to a *dolce far niente* from which it would not have been easy to emerge. Discipline is definitely one of the challenges and difficulties of autonomous group work. I promptly suggested we choose the theme on the use of computers in the School of Computing's teaching. This choice was accepted, and we went straight to the PC lab to make an assessment and audit of the various programs available on the computers. We counted around fifteen applications that we classified into different categories, such as word processors, spreadsheet and statistics packages, database systems, graphics tools, and programming language compilers software. We then decided to meet the following day to try and recruit a couple of more members and share the work.

The next afternoon, two more students joined us to complete the group. On my recommendation, Jonas was appointed the team leader, an opportunity for him to practise his leadership skills – and to learn how to take the blame if objectives are not met. Poor Jonas. In spite of his protestation, he was presented with a *fait accompli*. I must confess that I could not help feeling a certain *schadenfreude*, as I had imposed him as a candidate because I was afraid I would be saddled with the job, so I retrospectively begged for his forgiveness. Instead of leader of the group, I rather saw myself as its *éminence grise* – having all the benefits of power without, conveniently, any of the inconveniences. This is another feature of my pragmatic personality. Indeed, why complicate one's life?

We reviewed the various packages we had found the previous day and discussed the way to carry out this assignment. It was decided that each of us should examine one type of application, making comments on its efficiency in separate reports to be integrated into the final submission. I selected a programming language; one I was already familiar with. Computer systems consist of hardware – the physical and electronic parts – and software – the programs that reside in the memory and control each hardware component. And without programs, computers are useless. All programs are written in a programming language, a precise notation defining a sequence of instructions – the algorithm – to be processed and executed by a computer for a job to be completed successfully. In fact, there are two main types of software: application and system. Application software allows specific tasks to be executed; word processing, database, accounting or stock inventory systems would be examples of this. Whereas system software is responsible for managing and handling all hardware devices within a computer; the operating system being the critical program that monitors how the different parts of a computer operate together, as well as coordinating the diverse applications running. So, after each of us chose a specific package to work on, we agreed to meet at the end of the week to assess our progress.

In relation to our study of technology in our degree course, it is important to be aware of its function in communication. Today, we are witnessing an information revolution centred on the computer, yet few of us appreciate the extent to which it has changed our society and how much further this revolution still has to go. In the past couple of decades, the world has seen a revolution in the management of information: in the collection, storage, transfer, processing, usage, and presentation of data. And this revolution is as important in human history as was the industrial one of the nineteenth century. Ever since the Industrial Revolution, the requirement for timely and accurate mechanisms for information dissemination and distribution has grown, resulting in the development of machines that communicate with one another.

In fact, much of our modern society is based upon the communication of messages whose information content is generated by or through the use of machines. And the first of those apparatuses was the telegraph followed by the telephone, whose invention and development can be considered as the foundation of modern communication systems. Nowadays, the power of computers has been further enhanced by the development of networks, which link various pieces of hardware together in order to communicate with each other and share resources. Information moves around according to various communication protocols – set of rules that every computer follows to transfer data. For a device to communicate with another, both must speak the same language, otherwise communication is not possible, and it is these protocols that dictate which methods and instructions are used between computers during a communication session. Likewise in the case of distributed systems, for instance a collection of interconnected computers that coordinate their activities and communicate among themselves using message passing to solve complex computational problems that have been divided into smaller tasks assigned to one or more computers for processing, before a solution can be produced from the aggregate output sent back by the different nodes. An architecture having not only the benefit of better cost effectiveness over centralised mainframes or supercomputers, as it is based on commodity hardware – already available computing equipment – but also offers greater reliability – there is no single point of failure and in the event of a machine malfunction, the system as a whole is not compromised – and scalability – computing power can be increased relatively easily in small amounts.

This technology need not be complex and sophisticated in order to be effective, though. A medium such as radio can play a significant role in communities with deep oral traditions, where culture and knowledge are verbally transmitted across generations without a writing system. For example, in remote back country villages in Africa, many like to listen to old men and women telling the centuries-old tales of families and history. People have always loved hearing repeatedly stories about great chiefs, famous ancestors, or legendary clans; and although there were written languages in ancient Africa, the stories have been passed on orally from one generation to the next. And in these cultures, with a rich tapestry of oral customs such as storytelling, poetry recitation, singing and more, these elders, learned raconteurs, entertainers, and historians, have also been mediators between conflicting parties of their societies, thus having a role in advising, counselling, and trying to help people to live together peacefully. Listening to these sages, who are in reality living archives of verbal history, has always been an important social and cultural activity. But these wise men and women are dying out, and for the villagers the transistor radio, now cheaply available, has not only become the dominant source of information but also, in many cases, the main link with the rest of the world.

Telephone and broadcasting systems have become more versatile with improved performance. We can use the telephone to talk to people living on the other side of the world as easily as to those residing on the other side of the street. I believe, however, radio to be arguably the most powerful medium of mass communication as it is capable of reaching everyone, anywhere in the world, over long, medium, and short waves, with a minimum infrastructure. Electronic mail has now become increasingly popular, with many individuals and companies using this technology to communicate with friends, staff, colleagues, and clients, as it combines the advantages of the telephone for speed and spontaneity, with those of the letter for cost and clarity; also including scanned copies of documents that can be sent across the world in seconds.

We also have portable offices that fit in our palm; mobile phones and applications such as electronic mail are all coming together in a batch of hand-held computers. And these are connected to wireless networks for transmission to any part of the globe via satellite. Currently, 'personal digital assistants' are on the market, and we can appreciate that these devices, the size and weight of a small book – computers, as well as messengers – can easily communicate with the rest of the world. And, as time goes by, technophobes will happily continue to input data while riding the bus, sitting in a park, or going about town – even becoming gadget wizards capable of handling *le dernier cri* in communication technology. I remember an advertising slogan from a large public company saying we were never more than a phone call away. To that, thanks to the fast-growing network of international telecommunication, we could add that we are never more than a key stroke away.

NINTH WEEK

TENTH WEEK

ELEVENTH WEEK

To start this session, we reviewed the group project and discovered its purpose. By giving it to us, we were made aware of our responsibilities in the sense that we had to be able to coordinate our work with one accord. The importance of this aptitude was strongly emphasised because when we have our own careers, we most certainly will always be working with others. And we were also informed that subsequent classes would be dedicated to group skills. I do not fully subscribe to this notion that teamwork is indispensable, though I understand it is useful. Not being particularly fond of gatherings, I am not really gregarious, but rather more of an independently minded person, believing in the potential of the human individual. I know, as the Americans would say, that it takes a lot of chutzpah to make such a statement, but I am just more productive when I am able to make my own decisions and use my own initiative without arguing. That is not to say I cannot be part of a team. Occasionally, I work with me, myself, and my alter ego, but we always end up with conflicting ideas, taking on each other *mano a mano*, even when we manage to sit *tête-à-tête* – so I prefer working alone. Like a module within a computer program, I can interact with others but remain independent and in control of my performance. I am not saying that I am a staunch and unconditional individualist though. I am only implying it.

We then proceeded with writing a critical report on the presentation we gave a fortnight ago. It was an informal one in which we had to disclose our impressions on this event. I stated the problems encountered and made a general commentary outlining my feelings and observations, highlighting the issue we had in timing our talk and the challenges we faced in its preparation. Producing this assignment was the source of much hardship for many. Writing is so difficult because it is, above all, a thinking process. Writing is an intellectual strife demanding a general mobilisation of one's cerebral resources after neural drills done building strength of character and mental resistance against truly stressful opponents inducing nervous tension and emotional conflict, requiring morale fortitude with defensive concentration in defeating such soulful confrontations, followed by introspective missions and debriefing deliberations to assess subconscious deployment of imaginative troops and pondering artillery, disposed in accordance with reflective logistics and ingenious tactics elaborated during pensive reconnaissance over the meditative minefield, for intuitive objectives and inspirational targets to aim contemplative missiles and reasoning weapons discharging rational ammunition emulating inventive projectiles containing evocative explosives – before winning this psychological war with a triumphant spirit and a peace of mind.

A relentless personal campaign, waged as a combined operation to hunt down and neutralise mercilessly, with an arsenal of creativity, any menacing opposition located within range, obeying shoot-to-kill orders issued amid effective search-and-pursue policies developed over countless gruelling training exercises, performing complex precision manoeuvres perfectly executed with penetrating wit, to uncover the most insightful thought-provoking ideas, revealing any doubts and *arrière-pensées*, inflicting maximum devastation and heavy casualties on rival formations presenting the biggest threat at close quarters, eventually suppressing and sending them reeling back in retreat, unleashing salvos, including cannon balls, of originality. Then, pulling no punches, dodging challenging figurative bullets flying under the radar, displaying coolness under pressure and the will to survive, painstakingly infiltrating and conquering new territory inch by inch, demonstrating formidable resilience and resoluteness to secure key areas within the combat zone, distinguishing friend from foe to minimise collateral damage, avoiding potential pitfalls, seeking shelter in the face of danger, throwing idiomatic grenades around, and staying out of harm's way, while sticking to one's guns and standing one's ground. Exceptional heroism exemplifying valour at the front, gallantry in action, composure under fire, extreme devotion, loyalty to a cause and unflinching determination to achieve nothing less than total victory as the sole member of a highly disciplined autonomous elite commando unit. Anyhow, anywhere, anytime. The ultimate goal is finding, fixing, flanking and then finishing the enemy. And, with expert marksmanship, the writer's opinions caught in the crosshairs of deepening single-mindedness to define a line of sight, accomplish complete authorial occupation and establish full belletristic control over the work. The best of the very best.

A meritorious conduct deserving a medal of honour and citation in the form of a book, awarded for daring and preeminent service with conspicuous bravery above and beyond the call of duty, commendations praising and conferring that brilliant staff officer – recognising the importance of intrepidity and the advantage of superiority, having intimate knowledge of success or failure rests upon sound critical judgement based on accurate intelligence received from reliable and detailed situation awareness reports – promotion to the highest rank namely, supreme commander of joint allied cognitive forces, valiantly fighting on paper an epic armed struggle involving extraordinary difficult circumstances overcome implementing various contingency plans hinging on surprise preemptive strikes, offensive assaults, and decisive counterattacks in hostile terrain, magnificently delivering the *coup de grâce*, compelling entire adversary divisions to surrender unconditionally, even though rules of engagement state that no prisoners are taken by either belligerent side – the mother of all battles. And, as discussed earlier, given the proper occasion, with the help of computer simulation, energy released from thermonuclear fusion can be potentially transformed into a prodigious amount of literary power, the intensity of atomic words producing a blast enough to be blown away. Who would argue that the keyboard is not mightier than the sword? And how come I only lasted three days in the army? I am nonetheless a proud veteran, and I never fail to salute and thank myself for my sacrifice.

Talking, however, is much easier. One merely needs to open one's mouth and speak. On the subject of words, we have pondered over the languages of bodies, but what about the bodies of languages? Language is the most important and widespread of sign systems; all technology, civilisation, and culture depend upon it. Language – the communication of thoughts and feelings through a combination of signals such as voice sounds, gestures, or written symbols – may be used by a nation, a people, or a particular community. And in Western philosophy, language has long been closely associated with reason. The ability of human beings to store and to structure information, to think and solve problems, to engage in rational interaction with others, and to perceive the world in a purposeful way, is heavily dependent on their language capacity. Languages enable us to learn, to share information, and to communicate efficiently. Having visited places where I could not speak or read the local idiom, experiencing the inconvenience of limited functionality with my activities, feeling lost in a vacuum, and frustrated, I can appreciate how language is easily taken for granted. Without a common language, normal human life within a society is impossible.

Although there is every reason to believe English will continue to play the key role in global communication, I am well aware that, in this heterogeneous world, a knowledge of other languages can be very advantageous, especially if one plans to go abroad. For, in most other countries, English may be spoken in the major cities but that is not so true in the provinces and other remote regions, where the person who only understands this lingua franca misses out on so much, such as newspapers, books, cinema, and social contacts. I speak from personal experience, having lived in more countries than I can remember – like I said, I am a vagabond. As an atomic particle, I have been bouncing off different points in the world, spinning along divergent trajectories, incessantly moving around, with no stable position, setting on collision courses with random strangers and unpredictable events. I have invested time and effort to learn several other languages so as to make the most of my travels.

Born a foreigner in a foreign land and thus not belonging to any country, I am an international, multicultural, cosmopolitan, omnivorous sponge that absorbs and tries to appreciate all mores, outlooks, and philosophies encountered. I learn from the East and I learn from the West. Oriental philosophy of peace, patience and humility effectively complements Western technology, creativity and enterprise to achieve a harmonious equilibrium in life. The traditional can be combined with the modern, the spiritual with the material, and the theoretical with the practical. I tend to see myself as a cross between a virtual Marco Polo and Captain James Cook – navigator, traveller, and adventurer – often embarking, in a quest for knowledge and experience, on my own voyages of exploration and discovery of new ideas, cultures, and locations in the world, with a penchant for inspiration and enlightenment. Also, I have been influenced by the books I have read, the people I have met, and the places I have visited.

Being able to converse in the native tongue makes it easier to establish personal relationships and to understand the traditions and cultures of a country. I believe in the breaching of cultural barriers through mutual understanding and respect. As the Chinese philosopher Confucius once wrote:

'All people are the same – it is only their habits which are so different.' Outcasts, however, are different and have one advantage over others. Inferior by default, they make superior writers. Anyway, a blend of foreign words skillfully inserted into an English text with a strong *sprachgefühl* for diverse idioms can only enhance its beauty to a level commensurate with the status of world language par excellence.

In reference to the East, nothing in life is absolute, everything has both yin and yang features. Contrary forces, conflicting opinions, or disparate entities are all interconnected and interdependent, existing in relation to each other, complementary opposites interacting within a greater whole in the natural world. Fuzzy logic – reasoning that is loose and approximate rather than exact and fixed, recognising more than just true and false values – and chaos theory – dealing with complex, unpredictable and deterministic systems whose behaviour is decided by their initial conditions, trying to make sense of seemingly random data – both suggest we need to be able to embrace ambiguity, contradiction, and uncertainty – we should expect the unexpected. And, under quantum rules, an entity may persist in multiple states at the same time – known as the principle of superposition, the idea particles can exist in all possible states simultaneously. Order and chaos can often be hard to tell apart from apparent absurdity, confusion, and paradox as change happens in continuity. A dominant event within a relationship becomes non-dominant the next moment, before regaining its preeminent position after a certain period. Day comes after night as surely as night follows day. What goes up eventually comes down. Whenever a quality attains its maximum point or degree, it naturally begins to transform into the opposite attribute. Therefore, we should prefer probable and reasonable solutions to problems instead of dichotomous dogma, thus promoting the idea of balance. By avoiding extremes, not seeing the world in black and white, we can aim to find a middle ground.

The penultimate lecture began with a little exercise on group organisation. Chris asked us to form teams of five and gave us a theme on which to prepare a talk. We had ten minutes. In this space of time, we started debating among ourselves on how we could approach this task, deciding on the different subheadings each one of us would research. She told us that the aim of this activity was for us to practise meeting scheduling, as effective group work involves some organisational methodology. Among other things, we needed to introduce ourselves to one another before starting any discussion; we are also required to identify the key issues, asking everyone for opinions and ideas, and we must plan our time.

Afterwards, we viewed two videos relevant to the way sessions ought to be held. Some golden rules emerged – the focus of the group to avoid getting off the point – testing comprehension and making sure all the assertions have been understood – motivating the team by bringing in everyone who has something to say. Avoiding friction among a party is one of the chairperson's roles, as he or she should tactfully make sure the gathering gets on well. A few procedures taken in conference management are the determination of the assembly's purposes, of members' contributions, of the time limit, of the agenda, and the formulation of resolution minutes.

During the last class, we watched a programme on business letter writing. We were shown how to draft a business letter, especially one relating to a complication and requiring apologies, using a simple mnemonic rule: SCRAP – standing for 'Situation, Complication, Resolution, Action and Politeness'. In business, a letter is a permanent record; less casual than a telephone call, it can help explain or solve intermittent problems that arise. By following this simple pattern that outlines the order each section can be expressed in, we keep the letters short and to the point. Later, Valerie gave us some advice on how to conduct interviews and on how to exploit information from reference work; we also received sample questionnaire formats for doing surveys or handling interviews. And that concluded our series of lectures over the semester.

Throughout this module, the teaching team always tried to make us feel comfortable; they were encouraging from the very first day up to the last. Despite the anxiety causing the occasional frisson at the beginning, I had a very interesting time exploring various communication techniques, such as giving a presentation, using body language, and writing, the latter being the one I certainly used the most. As the exercises were practical, we could feel what we were learning. The syllabus was by no means exhaustive, but was sufficient for us to extrapolate from the course. I even applied physics and chemistry, as well as different mathematical concepts, including probability theory, and calculus, a method to calculate the rate of change – the derivative – of one quantity with respect to another. I covered a range of issues, also touching on quantum mechanics during the first week, when we crossed our paths and interfered with the direction of our diverging trajectories as we students met for the first time. And, I must admit that writing and compiling this communication file assignment has been a most challenging and fulfilling experience. Communication is about sending and receiving messages and targeting the right audience. Three channels of communication are used when interacting in person with others: the verbal – the words spoken, the vocal – the tone of voice, and the visual – body language.

If there is a fundamental concept associated with communication, it is *awareness*. Communication, in whatever form, is this magical feature that provides us with a general consciousness of the world around us – and of lands beyond. It enriches our lives, improves their quality, and gives us a better understanding of ourselves and of others. In the past, tragedies and atrocities occurred while a majority failed to know. Today, however, mass communication allows an unprecedented perspective of our environment. We are able to follow events unfolding in regions on the other side of the world as factually as if they were developing in our own country. An egocentric or apathetic attitude should therefore be less likely, in that, this high velocity of data flow now possible acquires a political and strategic dimension – the military calls it 'inhibition strategy'. Communication helps to bridge the gaps between continents, between nations, and between people, leaving no area *terra incognita*. Because, in short, if technology succeeds in shrinking our vast planet to the size of a small neighbourhood, as with components on a printed circuit board, on this earth we become just human elements all connected together. Directly or indirectly.

About the Author

Frederick David is an IT professional with many interests, including literature and writing. He is from nowhere and everywhere. After leading a peripatetic nomadic life and working in various casual jobs, he developed a keen interest in computing, before attending university to study for a computer degree course where this unique original piece of literary engineering was produced.

Having previously studied nuclear physics, his work defines a new genre in literature where, as an experimental physicist using particle physics and quantum mechanics, he attempts to transform atomic energy into significant literary power. In the process, he discovers that producing great literature is another possible application of harnessing nuclear fusion.

As David compiled his communication file that eventually evolved into this book, he recognised that of all methods of communication, writing was one he was the most comfortable and successful with by developing and shaping his personal opinions on a variety of questions and matters, while challenging his assumptions and pushing the boundaries of his understanding.

As a postgraduate from UK and Ireland universities, he continues to hone and improve his writing skills. With a holistic view on life and an inquisitive mind, he still likes to expand and broaden his education, acquiring and gaining further knowledge on countless subjects, specifically continuing to learn more about computing technology and programming, even beyond academia, as he considers himself to be an eternal and perpetual student. An average student.

Printed in Dunstable, United Kingdom

74070204R10068